**Editor**
Lorin E. Klistoff, M.A.

**Managing Editor**
Karen Goldfluss, M.S. Ed.

**Editor-in-Chief**
Sharon Coan, M.S. Ed.

**Cover Artist**
Barb Lorseyedi

**Art Director**
CJae Froshay

**Art Coordinator**
Kevin Barnes

**Imaging**
Temo Parra
Rosa C. See

**Product Manager**
Phil Garcia

**Publisher**
Mary D. Smith, M.S. Ed.

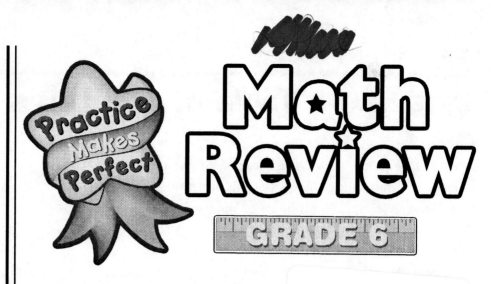

# Math Review

## GRADE 6

**Author**

*Mary Rosenberg*

***Teacher Created Resources, Inc.***
6421 Industry Way
Westminster, CA 92683
www.teachercreated.com

**ISBN-0-7439-3746-5**

*©2003 Teacher Created Resources, Inc.*
Reprinted, 2005
Made in U.S.A.

# Table of Contents

# ☙ Introduction ☙

The old adage "practice makes perfect" can really hold true for your child and his or her education. The more practice and exposure your child has with concepts being taught in school, the more success he or she is likely to find. For many parents, knowing how to help your children can be frustrating because the resources may not be readily available. As a parent it is also difficult to know where to focus your efforts so that the extra practice your child receives at home supports what he or she is learning in school.

This book has been designed to help parents and teachers reinforce basic skills with children. *Practice Makes Perfect* reviews basic math skills for children in grade 6. The focus is a review of math skills. While it would be impossible to include all concepts taught in grade 6 in this book, the following basic objectives are reinforced through practice exercises. These objectives support math standards established on a district, state, or national level. (Refer to Table of Contents for specific objectives of each practice page.)

- Working with numbers in the billions
- Working with integers
- Adding and subtracting positive and negative numbers
- Adding and subtracting fractions
- Finding the least common multiple
- Converting measurements
- Finding the mean, median, and mode

- Ordering operations
- Working with percentages
- Finding the interest
- Creating tables
- Finding the rate and volume
- Working with angles
- Solving algebraic equations

There are 36 practice pages. (*Note:* Have children show all work where computation is necessary to solve a problem. For multiple choice responses on practice pages, children can fill in the letter choice or circle the answer.) Following the practice pages are six test practices. These provide children with multiple-choice test items to help prepare them for standardized tests administered in schools. As your child completes each test, he or she can fill in the correct bubbles on the optional answer sheet provided on page 46. To correct the test pages and the practice pages in this book, use the answer key provided on pages 47 and 48.

## How to Make the Most of This Book

Here are some useful ideas for optimizing the practice pages in this book:

- Set aside a specific place in your home to work on the practice pages. Keep it neat and tidy with materials on hand.
- Set up a certain time of day to work on the practice pages. This will establish consistency. Look for times in your day or week that are less hectic and more conducive to practicing skills.
- Keep all practice sessions with your child positive and more constructive. If your child is having difficulty understanding what to do or how to get started, work through the first problem with him or her.
- Review the work your child has done. This serves as reinforcement and provides further practice.
- Pay attention to the areas in which your child has the most difficulty. Provide extra guidance and exercises in those areas. Allowing children to use drawings and manipulatives, such as coins, tiles, game markers, or flash cards, can help them grasp difficult concepts more easily.

# Practice 1

**Directions:** Read each word problem. Write a question for the missing piece of information.

1. Betsy is planning a party. She invited all of her friends. How many chairs does she need? _____

    _____

2. Each hen lays 1 egg a day. How many cartons of eggs do the hens lay each day? (1 carton = 12 eggs). _____

    _____

3. David is driving to the beach. His car gets 30 miles per gallon. How many gallons of gas does David need in order to drive to the beach and then back home?

    _____

    _____

4. The tickets at the local carnival cost $1.00 each. How many tickets can Suzanne buy with her weekly allowance? _____

    _____

5. Dad is baking cookies for the class party. He made 6 dozen cookies. How many cookies can each student have? _____

    _____

6. The bean plant grows an inch each day. How tall will the plant be at the end of the month? _____

    _____

7. Joanne ordered 8 boxes of markers. How many markers did Joanne order?

    _____

    _____

8. The bakery sells donuts for $0.25, pastries for $0.40, and coffee. How much does Bobby spend if he buys two donuts and a cup of coffee?

    _____

    _____

# Practice 2

**Directions:** Cross out the information that is not needed in order to solve the problem. Then solve the problem.

1. Ms. Johnson's beagle, Benny, eats 6 small dog bones each day. His favorite flavor of dog bones is peanut butter. How many dog bones does Benny eat in 5 weeks?



   Benny eats _____ dog bones in 5 weeks.


2. Mr. Snow has been collecting pennies for 80 years. He has collected $100 in pennies and $500 in nickels each year. How much money in pennies has Mr. Snow collected?



   Mr. Snow has collected _____ in pennies over 80 years.


3. Last week, at the Horse Race Arena, Arlene watched the final horse race of the season. The stadium was beautifully decorated. Tubby was the first place winner. He was given $1,200. Cubby placed second. He earned 25% less prize money than Tubby. How much money did Cubby receive?



   Cubby received _____ as the second place winner.


4. The mall has a huge parking garage. The parking garage was built in 1950. The garage has 4 levels. On each level 396 cars can park. How many cars does the parking garage hold?



   The parking garage can hold _____ cars.

# Practice 3

**Directions:** Add the missing commas to each number.

1. 2 7 7 4 3 8 5

2. 4 6 5 1 0 3 1 8 1

3. 2 5 8 6 8 1 0 7 5 5 9

4. 9 4 1 1 7 4 7 4 4 6 1 0

5. 3 7 1 0 1 6 9 7 1

6. 6 2 9 1 2 4 6 6 2 8

7. 2 9 8 6 9 5 4 9 3 1

8. 7 1 2 4 3 1 6 6 4

**Directions:** Write each number in standard form.

9. Four hundred twenty nine billion, one hundred one million, five hundred sixty-five thousand, four hundred eighty-six _____

10. Seven hundred twenty-five billion, one hundred eight million, three hundred twenty-eight thousand, five hundred fourteen _____

11. Eight hundred ninety-seven billion, one hundred twenty-nine million, one hundred eighty-four thousand, one hundred ten _____

12. One hundred seven billion, seven hundred seventy-two million, one hundred six thousand, seven hundred sixty-one _____

**Directions:** Write each number in expanded form using numbers.

**Example:** 541,867,935,584

500,000,000,000 + 40,000,000,000 + 1,000,000,000 + 800,000,000 + 60,000,000 + 7,000,000 + 900,000 + 30,000 + 5,000 + 500 + 80 + 4

13. 331,938,547,446 _____

_____

_____

_____

14. 695,665,839,720 _____

_____

_____

_____

# Practice 4

**Directions:** Write the actual problem. Estimate by rounding each number to the nearest ten thousand. Then solve the estimated problem. Solve the actual problem and answer the question.

- If the number in the thousands place is <u>5 or more</u>, round up.
- If the number in the thousands place is <u>less than 5</u>, round down.

| Problem | Actual | Estimated |
|---|---|---|
| **1.** 69,109 people attended the exhibit on Saturday and 55,318 people attended the exhibit on Sunday. How many people in all saw the exhibit? | 69,109<br>+ 55,318<br><br>Was the estimate reasonable?<br>Yes    No | _____<br>+ _____ |
| **2.** 63,549 people attended the concert last week. 55,318 people attended the concert this week. Find the difference between the two attendance figures. | _____<br>– _____<br><br>Was the estimate reasonable?<br>Yes    No | _____<br>– _____ |
| **3.** 77,352 people watched the football game. 31,166 people watched the basketball game. How many people in all watched a sporting event? | _____<br>+ _____<br><br>Was the estimate reasonable?<br>Yes    No | _____<br>+ _____ |
| **4.** 88,818 people walked across the bridge. 8,167 people biked across the bridge. Find the difference between the two methods of transportation. | _____<br>– _____<br><br>Was the estimate reasonable?<br>Yes    No | _____<br>– _____ |

# Practice 5

**Directions:** Integers are whole positive numbers or whole negative numbers. Circle the integers in each row.

| | | | | | |
|---|---|---|---|---|---|
| **1.** | 17 | 5/6 | .96 | 51% | ⁻35/40 |
| **2.** | ⁻54 | ⁻61 | ⁻3/2 | ⁺25 | .45 |
| **3.** | ⁻.22 | 17% | 9.4 | ⁻19 | 10/100 |
| **4.** | 3 7/10 | 40 | ⁻29 | 15.20 | 98 |

**Directions:** Use the number line to locate a number and to determine if the number is negative or positive. Write + (positive) or – (negative) before each number. The first one has been done for you.

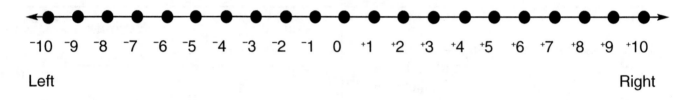

⁻10 ⁻9 ⁻8 ⁻7 ⁻6 ⁻5 ⁻4 ⁻3 ⁻2 ⁻1 0 ⁺1 ⁺2 ⁺3 ⁺4 ⁺5 ⁺6 ⁺7 ⁺8 ⁺9 ⁺10

Left                                                                 Right

**5.** One number to the left of 8 is \_\_\_\_⁺7\_\_\_\_.

**6.** Ten numbers to the left of 5 is _____.

**7.** Four numbers to the left of 5 is _____.

**8.** Four numbers to the left of 10 is _____.

**9.** Seven numbers to the right of 2 is _____.

**10.** Two numbers to the left of 4 is _____.

**11.** Five numbers to the left of 0 is _____.

**12.** Three numbers to the left of 2 is _____.

# Practice 6

**Directions:** Complete the number line.

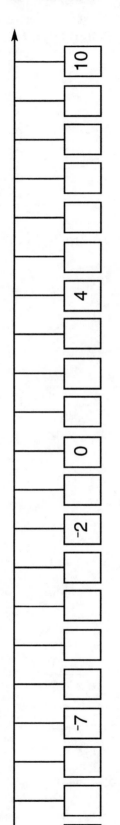

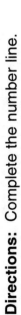

**Directions:** Write the following numbers in order from smallest to the greatest.

1. $^-3$, $^-4$, $5$, $^-9$, $^-7$

_____

2. $8$, $^-3$, $5$, $9$, $^-1$

_____

3. $^-6$, $^-10$, $^-3$, $1$, $3$

_____

4. $^-2$, $5$, $^-8$, $0$, $4$

_____

5. $2$, $^-9$, $^-6$, $1$, $^-8$

_____

6. $^-1$, $4$, $3$, $^-6$, $^-7$

_____

7. $10$, $^-6$, $2$, $0$, $^-5$

_____

# Practice 7

**Directions:** Circle the problems where a negative number is added to the first number.

1. ⁻9 + ⁻7    2. ⁻10 + ⁻2    3. 5 + 4    4. 2 − ⁻2

5. 3 + ⁻8    6. 9 + 3    7. 7 − ⁺9    8. ⁻3 − ⁻2

9. ⁻10 + ⁻7    10. 9 + ⁻2    11. ⁻10 − ⁺3    12. 2 − ⁺9

**Directions:** Draw a line under the problems where a negative number is subtracted from the first number.

13. 4 + ⁻7    14. ⁻4 − 7    15. ⁻6 − ⁻7    16. 1 + ⁻9

17. ⁻8 + 4    18. 0 − ⁻5    19. 5 − ⁺4    20. ⁻10 + ⁻6

21. 9 + ⁻8    22. 4 − ⁺10    23. ⁻5 − ⁻1    24. 5 − ⁺5

**Directions:** Solve each problem.

25. ⁻5 − ⁻2 = _____    26. ⁻6 − 6 = _____    27. ⁻9 + ⁻8 = _____

28. 6 − 4 = _____    29. ⁻10 + 5 = _____    30. 5 − 1 = _____

31. 8 + 9 = _____    32. ⁻2 + 7 = _____    33. ⁻9 + ⁻6 = _____

34. 4 − ⁺9 = _____    35. ⁻4 − ⁻7 = _____    36. 7 − ⁺1 = _____

37. 10 − ⁻4 = _____    38. ⁻8 + ⁻2 = _____    39. ⁻9 + 2 = _____

40. 7 − ⁺8 = _____    41. 6 − ⁺6 = _____    42. 4 − ⁻7 = _____

# Practice 8

**Directions:** Find the least (or smallest) common multiple for each set of numbers. Write the least common multiple like this: LCM (3, 4) = 12.

1.  5: _____

    6: _____          LCM (5, 6) = _____

2.  3: _____

    7: _____          LCM (3, 7) = _____

3.  8: _____

    9: _____          LCM (8, 9) = _____

**Directions:** Find the prime factors for each number. Multiply the factors to find the least common multiple for each set of numbers. Write the least common multiple like this: LCM (4, 5) = 20.

4.  9: _____

    14: _____          LCM (9, 14) = _____

5.  12: _____

    5: _____          LCM (12, 5) = _____

6.  10: _____

    3: _____          LCM (10, 3) = _____

7.  15: _____

    2: _____          LCM (15, 2) = _____

8.  8: _____

    21: _____          LCM (8, 21) = _____

# Practice 9

**Directions:** Add or subtract. Some fractions may need to be renamed. Reduce the answer to its simplest form.

| | | |
|---|---|---|
| **1.** $\begin{array}{r} 2\frac{3}{10} \\ +\ 3\frac{5}{10} \\ \hline \end{array}$ | **2.** $\begin{array}{r} 6\frac{7}{10} \\ +\ 8\frac{3}{10} \\ \hline \end{array}$ | **3.** $\begin{array}{r} 9\frac{2}{5} \\ +\ 6\frac{1}{5} \\ \hline \end{array}$ |
| **4.** $\begin{array}{r} 9\frac{1}{6} \\ -\ 5\frac{3}{6} \\ \hline \end{array}$ | **5.** $\begin{array}{r} 7\frac{7}{8} \\ -\ 4\frac{4}{8} \\ \hline \end{array}$ | **6.** $\begin{array}{r} 4\frac{1}{11} \\ +\ 7\frac{10}{11} \\ \hline \end{array}$ |
| **7.** $\begin{array}{r} 8\frac{3}{9} \\ -\ 5\frac{1}{9} \\ \hline \end{array}$ | **8.** $\begin{array}{r} 7\frac{9}{10} \\ +\ 3\frac{9}{10} \\ \hline \end{array}$ | **9.** $\begin{array}{r} 10\frac{3}{8} \\ -\ 4\frac{7}{8} \\ \hline \end{array}$ |

# Practice 10

**Directions:** Add or subtract. Reduce the answer to its simplest form or rewrite as a mixed fraction.

| | | | |
|---|---|---|---|
| **1.** $+\dfrac{\dfrac{1}{10}}{\dfrac{4}{12}}$ | **2.** $-\dfrac{\dfrac{2}{4}}{\dfrac{1}{8}}$ | **3.** $-\dfrac{\dfrac{11}{12}}{\dfrac{4}{9}}$ | **4.** $+\dfrac{\dfrac{5}{11}}{\dfrac{4}{8}}$ |
| **5.** $-\dfrac{\dfrac{10}{11}}{\dfrac{1}{2}}$ | **6.** $+\dfrac{\dfrac{5}{8}}{\dfrac{8}{11}}$ | **7.** $-\dfrac{\dfrac{3}{5}}{\dfrac{3}{12}}$ | **8.** $+\dfrac{\dfrac{2}{3}}{\dfrac{3}{4}}$ |
| **9.** $9\dfrac{10}{12}$ $-5\dfrac{6}{7}$ | **10.** $4\dfrac{5}{7}$ $-4\dfrac{1}{12}$ | **11.** $8\dfrac{5}{10}$ $-4\dfrac{2}{8}$ | **12.** $8\dfrac{5}{6}$ $-1\dfrac{4}{5}$ |
| **13.** $10\dfrac{3}{7}$ $+2\dfrac{6}{10}$ | **14.** $3\dfrac{3}{6}$ $-2\dfrac{3}{4}$ | **15.** $1\dfrac{6}{8}$ $+3\dfrac{2}{6}$ | **16.** $8\dfrac{4}{7}$ $+3\dfrac{2}{10}$ |

# Practice 11

**Directions:** Solve each problem. Use the answers to decode the mystery message.

| 1.   A | 2.   B | 3.   E | 4.   G | 5.   I | 6.   L | 7.   M |
|--------|--------|--------|--------|--------|--------|--------|
| 610 <br> x 100 | 3 <br> x 100 | 724 <br> x 10 | 100 <br> x 56 | 100 <br> x 918 | 10 <br> x 571 | 385 <br> x 1,000 |

| 8.   N | 9.   P | 10.   S | 11.   T | 12.   U | 13.   Y | |
|--------|--------|---------|---------|---------|---------|--|
| 100 <br> x 410 | 726 <br> x 1,000 | 881 <br> x 10 | 37 <br> x 1,000 | 9 <br> x 1,000 | 0 <br> x 1,000 | |

___ ___ ___ ___ ___ ___ ___ ___ ___ ___ ___
385,000  9,000  5,710  37,000  91,800  726,000  5,710  0  91,800  41,000  5,600

___ ___ ___ ___ ___ ___
300  0  37,000  7,240  41,000  8,810

___ ___ ___ ___ ___ ___!
91,800  8,810  7,240  61,000  8,810  0

**Directions:** Write the >, <, or = sign in the circle

| 14. 745 x 100 ◯ 289 x 10 | 15. 10 x 10 ◯ 90 x 100 |
|---|---|
| 16. 88 x 1,000 ◯ 52 x 10 | 17. 5 x 1,000 ◯ 413 x 10 |
| 18. 100 x 79 ◯ 1,000 x 21 | 19. 41 x 100 ◯ 1,000 x 18 |

 *#3746 Practice Makes Perfect: Math Review*

# Practice 12

## Supply Room Inventory

| | | | |
|---|---|---|---|
| **pencils** <br> 68 per box | **erasers** <br> 847 per box | **crayons** <br> 271 per box | **markers** <br> 199 per box |
| **rulers** <br> 952 per box | **notepads** <br> 88 per box | **hole punches** <br> 348 per box | **binders** <br> 17 per box |
| **pens** <br> 1,107 per box | **rubber bands** <br> 23 per box | **sheets of paper** <br> 7,127 per box | **folders** <br> 1,104 per box |

**Directions:** Use the chart to write and solve each problem. The first one has been done for you.

| 1. 61 boxes of rulers <br><br> $\begin{array}{r} 952 \\ \times\ 61 \\ \hline 952 \\ +\ 57,120 \\ \hline 58,072 \end{array}$ | 2. 37 boxes of pencils | 3. 58 boxes of binders | 4. 759 boxes of erasers |
|---|---|---|---|
| 5. 373 boxes of notepads | 6. 19 boxes of pens | 7. 99 boxes of rubber bands | 8. 314 boxes of hole punches |
| 9. 510 boxes of paper | 10. 217 boxes of markers | 11. 71 boxes of crayons | 12. 861 boxes of folders |

# Practice 13 ♪ ☙ ♪ ☙ ♪ ☙ ♪ ☙ ♪ ☙ ♪ ☙ ♪ ♪ ☙

**Directions:** Find the product.

| | | | |
|---|---|---|---|
| **1.** <br> 4,511 <br> x 12 | **2.** <br> 8,476 <br> x 34 | **3.** <br> 7,386 <br> x 18 | **4.** <br> 4,156 <br> x 18 |
| **5.** <br> 32,566 <br> x 145 | **6.** <br> 54,373 <br> x 810 | **7.** <br> 36,592 <br> x 484 | **8.** <br> 65,349 <br> x 785 |
| **9.** <br> 175,797 <br> x 153 | **10.** <br> 412,699 <br> x 328 | **11.** <br> 297,365 <br> x 105 | **12.** <br> 567,899 <br> x 346 |

**Directions:** Use <, >, or = symbols to compare each set of numbers.

| | |
|---|---|
| **13.** 101 x 73 ◯ 331 x 68 | **14.** 972 x 75 ◯ 594 x 588 |
| **15.** 1,029 x 81 ◯ 615 x 421 | **16.** 839 x 771 ◯ 4,492 x 24 |
| **17.** 8,126 x 371 ◯ 42,313 x 62 | **18.** 58,648 x 495 ◯ 6,915 x 370 |

# Practice 14

**Directions:** Write the division problem and solve. Multiply to check the answer. The first one has been done for you.

| | | |
|---|---|---|
| **1.** 8,400 cookies divided into 40 boxes<br><br>**Check:**<br><br>$$\begin{array}{r} 210 \\ 40\overline{)8400} \\ -\,80 \\ \hline 40 \\ -\,40 \\ \hline 00 \end{array}$$  $$\begin{array}{r} 210 \\ \times\,40 \\ \hline 000 \\ +8,400 \\ \hline 8,400 \end{array}$$ | **2.** 41,916 pieces of bubble gum divided into 28 cartons<br><br><br>**Check:** | **3.** 33,320 decks of playing cards divided into 136 cases<br><br><br>**Check:** |
| **4.** 3,600 marbles placed into 90 pouches<br><br><br><br>**Check:** | **5.** 8,928 potato chips placed into 9 gigantic bowls<br><br><br><br>**Check:** | **6.** 28,917 game pieces for 81 board games<br><br><br><br>**Check:** |
| **7.** 35,620 paper clips placed into 260 canisters<br><br><br><br>**Check:** | **8.** 180,930 ants in 37 colonies<br><br><br><br>**Check:** | **9.** 8,840 peanuts for 65 elephants<br><br><br><br>**Check:** |

# Practice 15 ೨ ☙ ೨ ☙ ೨ ☙ ೨ ☙ ೨ ☙ ೨ ☙ ೨ ☙ ೨ ☙

**Directions:** Solve each problem.

| | | | |
|---|---|---|---|
| **1.** $123\overline{)79{,}154}$ | **2.** $24\overline{)67{,}398}$ | **3.** $31\overline{)59{,}743}$ | **4.** $17\overline{)31{,}064}$ |
| **5.** $10\overline{)38{,}761}$ | **6.** $85\overline{)93{,}752}$ | **7.** $658\overline{)78{,}216}$ | **8.** $910\overline{)29{,}176}$ |
| **9.** $465\overline{)65{,}674}$ | **10.** $153\overline{)213{,}657}$ | **11.** $619\overline{)341{,}750}$ | **12.** $313\overline{)2{,}425{,}401}$ |
| **13.** $92\overline{)299{,}189}$ | **14.** $378\overline{)51{,}627}$ | **15.** $105\overline{)748{,}294}$ | **16.** $110\overline{)1{,}364{,}106}$ |

# Practice 16

**Directions:** Complete the chart.

|     | Hours | Minutes | Seconds |
| --- | --- | --- | --- |
| **1.** | 1/4 | | |
| **2.** | 1/2 | | |
| **3.** | 3/4 | | |
| **4.** | 1 | | |
| **5.** | 2 | | |
| **6.** | 3 | | |
| **7.** | 4 | | |
| **8.** | 6 | | |
| **9.** | 8 | | |
| **10.** | 12 | | |
| **11.** | 18 | | |
| **12.** | 24 | | |

**Directions:** Use the >, <, or = symbols to compare each pair of times.

| | |
| --- | --- |
| **13.** 210 seconds ◯ 2 minutes | **14.** 98 minutes ◯ 5 hours |
| **15.** 27 minutes ◯ 630 seconds | **16.** 4 hours ◯ 6,641 seconds |

# Practice 17

**Equivalents**
12 inches = 1 foot
36 inches = 1 yard
3 feet = 1 yard

**Directions:** Write the number of inches.

**1.** 7 feet = _____ inches

**2.** 5 feet = _____ inches

**3.** 2 feet = _____ inches

**4.** 10 feet = _____ inches

**5.** 5 1/2 feet = _____ inches

**6.** 2 1/4 feet =_____ inches

**7.** 6 1/2 feet = _____ inches

**8.** 5 2/3 feet = _____ inches

**Directions:** Write the number of feet.

**9.** 96 inches = _____ feet

**10.** 12 inches = _____ foot

**11.** 24 inches = _____ feet

**12.** 48 inches = _____ feet

**13.** 68 inches = _____ feet

**14.** 6 inches = _____ foot

**15.** 30 inches = _____ feet

**16.** 54 inches = _____ feet

**Directions:** Write the number of yards.

**17.** 24 feet = _____ yards

**18.** 6 feet = _____ yards

**19.** 12 feet = _____ yards

**20.** 7 feet = _____ yards

**21.** 72 inches = _____ yards

**22.** 36 inches = _____ yard

# Practice 18

| Weekly Allowances | | | | | |
|---|---|---|---|---|---|
| Jordan | $9.00 | Charles | $7.00 | Misty | $1.00 |
| Davia | $2.00 | Billy | $4.00 | Sherry | $9.00 |
| Michelle | $9.00 | David | $6.00 | Bernice | $7.00 |
| Stan | $2.00 | | | | |

**1. Mean** is the average allowance. To find the mean add the total amount of money paid divided by the number of kids. What is the average weekly allowance?

The average weekly allowance is _____.

**2. Median** is the middle score between the highest amount and the lowest amount. If there are an even number of amounts in the range, add the two middle amounts together and divide by two to find the median. What is the median amount?

Lowest Amount                                           Highest Amount

The median amount is _____.

# Practice 19

**Weekly Allowances**

| Jordan | $9.00 | Charles | $7.00 | Misty | $1.00 |
|--------|-------|---------|-------|-------|-------|
| Davia | $2.00 | Billy | $4.00 | Sherry | $9.00 |
| Michelle | $9.00 | David | $6.00 | Bernice | $7.00 |
| Stan | $2.00 | | | | |

1. **Mode** is the amount that occurs most frequently. Make a graph showing the different amounts of money. What is the mode?

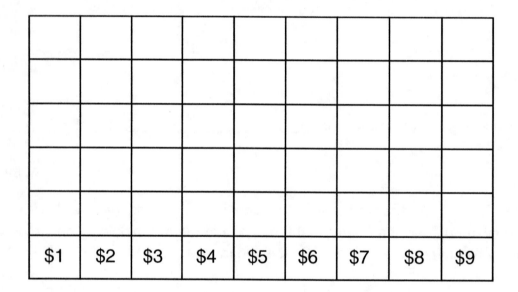

| $1 | $2 | $3 | $4 | $5 | $6 | $7 | $8 | $9 |

The mode is _____.

2. What would happen to the mean if Misty and Charles had their allowances doubled?

_____

3. What would happen to the mode if 5 kids received $5.00 allowances and 5 kids received $10.00 allowances? _____

# Practice 20

### Order of Operations
1. Parentheses
2. Exponents
3. Multiply/divide from left to right
4. Add/subtract from left to right

**Directions:** Solve each problem.

| | | |
|---|---|---|
| **1.**<br><br>10 + (8 x 2) = _____ | **2.**<br><br>(1 x 3) + 26 = _____ | **3.**<br><br>(10 ÷ 5) − 2 = _____ |
| **4.**<br>(9 ÷ 3) + 9 − 10 = _____ | **5.**<br>5 + (6 x 7) − 3 =_____ | **6.**<br>(5 x 4) + 3 − 4 = _____ |
| **7.**<br>$(4^2 + 5) ÷ 3$ = _____ | **8.**<br>$(8 + 9) − (9 − 2^2)$ = _____ | **9.**<br>(1 x 1) + (6 x 6) = _____ |
| **10.**<br>(24 ÷ 8) x 3 − 7 = _____ | **11.**<br>8(7 ÷ 7) + 2 = _____ | **12.**<br>$(4^2 + 3^3) − 40$ = _____ |

# Practice 21 ð ❦ ð ❦ ð ❦ ð ❦ ð ❦ ð ❦ ð ❦ ð ❦

**Directions:** Find each student's spelling score. Round each score to the nearest whole percentage point. The first one has been done for you.

| | | | |
|---|---|---|---|
| **1.** Josh had 1 out of 8 words correct.<br><br>$$\begin{array}{r} .125 \\ 8\overline{)1.000} \\ -8 \phantom{00}\\ \hline 20 \phantom{0}\\ -16 \phantom{0}\\ \hline 40 \\ 40 \\ \hline 0 \end{array}$$ | **2.** Nicole had 3 out of 9 words correct. | **3.** Eric had 8 out of 9 words correct. | **4.** Brandi had 1 out of 6 words correct. |
| **5.** Monica had 1 out of 2 words correct. | **6.** Rob had 6 out of 7 words correct. | **7.** J.R. had 2 out of 7 words correct. | **8.** Sue Ellen had 4 out of 5 words correct. |

9. Which student had the highest spelling score? _____

10. Which student had the lowest spelling score? _____

**Directions:** Find the number of spelling words each student spelled correctly. The first one has been done for you.

| | |
|---|---|
| **11.** Donnie spelled 15% of 20 words correctly.<br><br>.15 x 20 = 3<br><br>Donnie spelled _____ words correctly. | **12.** Sammy spelled 40% of 5 words correctly.<br><br><br><br>Sammy spelled _____ words correctly. |
| **13.** Jessica spelled 75% of 4 words correctly.<br><br><br><br>Jessica spelled _____ words correctly. | **14.** Ashley spelled 35% of 20 words correctly.<br><br><br><br>Ashley spelled _____ words correctly. |

# Practice 22 ✎ ☙ ✎ ☙ ✎ ☙ ✎ ☙ ✎ ☙ ✎ ☙ ✎ ☙

**Directions:** Find the number of correct answers. Round to the nearest whole number.

1. There were 5 questions on the test. Niles answered 80% of them correctly.

   Niles answered _____ questions correctly.

2. There were 12 questions on the test. Samantha answered 75% of them correctly.

   Samantha answered _____ questions correctly.

3. There were 10 questions on the history test. Davey answered 60% of them correctly.

   Davey answered _____ questions correctly.

4. There were 20 questions on the test. Sally answered 25% of them correctly.

   Sally answered _____ questions correctly.

5. There were 40 questions on the social studies test. Daniel answered 90% of them correctly.

   Daniel answered _____ questions correctly.

6. There were 12 questions on the test. Cindy answered 50% of them correctly.

   Cindy answered _____ questions correctly.

**Directions:** Find the number. Round to the nearest whole number.

| | | |
|---|---|---|
| **7.** 35% of 25 = _____ | **8.** 15% of 12 = _____ | **9.** 5% of 100 = _____ |
| **10.** 50% of 26 = _____ | **11.** 10% of 80 = _____ | **12.** 70% of 15 = _____ |

# Practice 23

| The People's Bank | | | |
|---|---|---|---|
| (Interest earned per month) | | | |
| $25–$250 | No Interest | $751–$1,000 | 2% |
| $251–$500 | 1% | $1,001–$10,000 | 3% |
| $501–$750 | 1.5% | More than $10,000 | 3.5% |

**Directions:** Use the chart to find the interest earned on each savings account.

Jamie opens a savings account with $1,500.00. She leaves the money in the account for 1 month.

**1.** How much interest does she earn? _____

**2.** What is her ending balance? _____

Lee opens a savings account with $250.00. Lee leaves the money in the account for 2 months.

**3.** How much interest does Lee earn the first month? _____

**4.** How much interest does Lee earn the second month? _____

**5.** What do you notice about answers 3 and 4? _____

_____

Suppose Lee adds $100 to the account at the beginning of the second month.

**6.** How much interest would Lee earn? _____

**7.** How much money would Lee have in the account? _____

Curtis opens a savings account with $5,000. He leaves the money in the bank for 1 month.

**8.** How much interest does he earn? _____

**9.** What is his ending balance? _____

# Practice 24 ⟨swirl decorations⟩

**Directions:** Lance received a credit card in the mail. He charged $500.00. Figure out how much that $500.00 really costs!

---

### U-Can-Charge-It Credit Card

20% Interest Each Month
$50.00 Minimum Monthly Payment

---

**1.** Suppose Lance only makes the minimum payment each month for 4 months.

| Month | Beginning Balance | + 20% Interest | – Payment | Ending Balance |
|-------|-------------------|----------------|-----------|----------------|
| 1 | $500.00 | + $100.00 | – $50.00 | $550.00 |
| 2 | $550.00 | | | |
| 3 | | | | |
| 4 | | | | |
| 5 | | | | |

**2.** What would happen if Lance continued to make only the minimum payment each month?

_____

_____

**3.** Would Lance ever be able to pay off the balance? Why or why not?

_____

**4.** How much interest would Lance have paid over 4 months? _____

---

# Practice 25 ﾐ ﾐ ﾐ ﾐ ﾐ ﾐ ﾐ ﾐ ﾐ ﾐ ﾐ ﾐ ﾐ ﾐ ﾐ

**Directions:** Lance received a credit card in the mail. He charged $500.00. Figure out how much that $500.00 really costs!

---

### U-Can-Charge-It Credit Card

20% Interest Each Month
$50.00 Minimum Monthly Payment

---

1. Suppose Lance pays $200.00 each month on the balance.

| Month | Beginning Balance | + 20% Interest | – Payment | Ending Balance |
|:-----:|:-----------------:|:--------------:|:---------:|:--------------:|
| 1 | $500.00 | + $100.00 | – $200.00 | $400.00 |
| 2 | $400.00 | | | |
| 3 | | | | |
| 4 | | | | |
| 5 | | | | |

2. How much interest would he have paid to pay off the original $500.00 charge?

   _____

3. What is the total amount Lance would have paid (the $500 charged plus the interest)?

   _____

4. If Lance had put the $500.00 in a savings account paying 5% interest each month, how much interest would he have earned over the course of 4 months? _____

5. Find the difference between the interest Lance could have earned in a savings account and the interest Lance paid on the credit card. The difference is _____.

# Practice 26 ⟋ ⟋ ⟋ ⟋ ⟋ ⟋ ⟋ ⟋ ⟋ ⟋ ⟋ ⟋ ⟋

**Directions:** Use the information to create the table.

1. Jason packs eggs at a rate of 2 cartons every 3 minutes.

| Cartons | Minutes |
|---------|---------|
|         |         |
|         |         |
|         |         |
|         |         |
|         |         |
|         |         |

2. Sheryl can read 5 words every 12 seconds.

| Words | Seconds |
|-------|---------|
|       |         |
|       |         |
|       |         |
|       |         |
|       |         |
|       |         |

3. Roscoe can stamp 30 envelopes to Rita's 10 licking envelopes.

| Stamping | Licking |
|----------|---------|
|          |         |
|          |         |
|          |         |
|          |         |
|          |         |
|          |         |

4. Louisa can do 3 jumping jacks to Marvin's 2 sit-ups.

| Jumping Jacks | Sit-Ups |
|---------------|---------|
|               |         |
|               |         |
|               |         |
|               |         |
|               |         |
|               |         |

# Practice 27 ⟋ ⟍ ⟋ ⟍ ⟋ ⟍ ⟋ ⟍ ⟋ ⟍ ⟋ ⟍ ⟋ ⟍

**Directions:** *Rate* tells the measure of one quantity as it relates to the value of another quantity. Find the rate. The first one has been done for you.

---

**1.** Bill can walk 3 miles in 45 minutes. How long will it take Bill to walk 10 miles?

$$\frac{1}{15} \frac{\cancel{3} \text{ miles}}{\cancel{45} \text{ min.}} = \frac{10 \text{ miles}}{n}$$

It will take Bill ___150___ minutes.

---

**2.** Marcie can jog a mile every 6 minutes. How many miles can Marcie jog in 30 minutes?

Marcie can jog _____ miles.

---

**3.** Andrew can rollerblade 1 block every 15 seconds. How many blocks can Andrew rollerblade in 2 minutes?

Andrew can rollerblade _____ blocks.

---

**4.** Mona drove 40 miles per hour. How long will it take Mona to drive 100 miles?

It will take Mona _____ hours.

---

**5.** The airplane flies 725 miles per hour. How many minutes will it take the plane to fly 150 miles?

It will take the plane _____ minutes.

---

**6.** It takes Olivia 30 seconds to count to 25. How many minutes will it take Olivia to count to 300?

It will take Olivia _____ minutes.

---

# Practice 28

**Directions:** Find the volume for each rectangular solid.

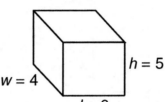

> ## Volume Formula
>
> *length* x *width* x *height* = cubic units
>
> V = *l* x *w* x *h*

**1.**

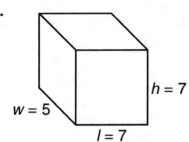

h = 7
w = 5
l = 7

_____ x _____ x _____ =

_____ cubic units

**2.**

h = 5
w = 4
l = 6

_____ x _____ x _____ =

_____ cubic units

**3.**

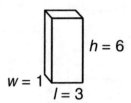

h = 6
w = 1
l = 3

_____ x _____ x _____ =

_____ cubic units

**Directions:** Find the volume for each cube.

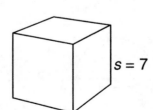

> ## Volume Formula
>
> *side* x *side* x *side* = cubic units
>
> V = s³

**4.**

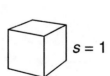

s = 1

_____³ = _____ cubic units

**5.**

s = 7

_____³ = _____ cubic units

**6.**

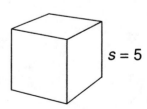

s = 5

_____³ = _____ cubic units

# Practice 29

**Directions:** Find the volume for each cylinder.

> ## Volume Formula
>
> *pi* x *radius* x *radius* x *height*
>
> $V = 3.14 \times r^2 \times h$

**1.**

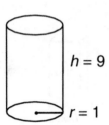

$h = 9$

$r = 1$

The volume is

_____ cubic units.

**2.**

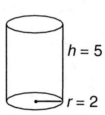

$h = 5$

$r = 2$

The volume is

_____ cubic units.

**3.**

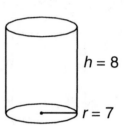

$h = 8$

$r = 7$

The volume is

_____ cubic units.

**Directions:** Find the volume for each sphere.

> ## Volume Formula
>
> 4/3 x *pi* x *r* x *r* x *r* = cubic units
>
> $V = 4/3 \times 3.14 \times r^3$

**4.**

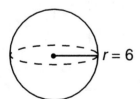

$r = 6$

The volume is

_____ cubic units.

**5.**

$r = 2$

The volume is

_____ cubic units.

**6.**

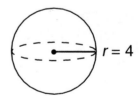

$r = 4$

The volume is

_____ cubic units.

# Practice 30

**Directions:** Match each word to its definition.

| | | |
|---|---|---|
| **1.** acute | 90° angle |
| **2.** equilateral | no congruent sides |
| **3.** isosceles | three congruent sides |
| **4.** obtuse | angle less than 90° |
| **5.** right | two congruent sides |
| **6.** scalene | angle more than 90° |

**Directions:** Describe each triangle by its number of congruent sides and by its angle.

| **Congruent sides:** | scalene | equilateral | isosceles |
|---|---|---|---|
| **Angles:** | acute | right | obtuse |

**7.**

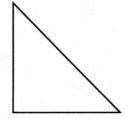

_____

_____

**8.**

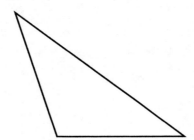

_____

_____

**9.**

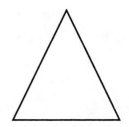

_____

_____

# Practice 31

**Directions:** Use a protractor to measure each angle.

**1.**

angle = _____ °

**2.**

angle = _____ °

**3.**

angle = _____ °

**4.**

angle = _____ °

**5.**

angle = _____ °

**6.**

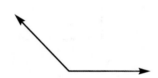

angle = _____ °

**7.**

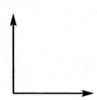

angle = _____ °

**8.**

angle = _____ °

**9.**

angle = _____ °

# Practice 32

**Directions:** Name each angle two ways.

**1.**

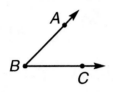

_____

_____

**2.**

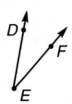

_____

_____

**3.**

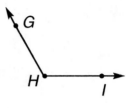

_____

_____

**Directions:** Name each pair of adjacent angles.

**4.**

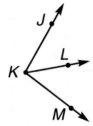

_____ and _____

**5.**

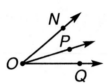

_____ and _____

**6.**

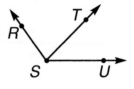

_____ and _____

**Directions:** Write *perpendicular* or *intersecting*.

**7.**

_____

**8.**

_____

**9.**

_____

**Directions:** Write *supplementary* or *complementary*.

**10.**

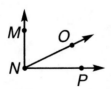

∠ MNO and ∠ONP

are _____.

**11.**

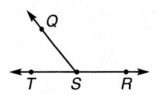

∠TSQ and ∠QSR

are _____.

# Practice 33

**Directions:** Use a protractor to draw the following angles.

**1.** 120°

**2.** 75°

**3.** 50°

**4.** 140°

**5.** 175°

**6.** 5°

**7.** 20°

**8.** 100°

**9.** 160°

**10.** 25°

# Practice 34

**Directions:** Solve for *x*. Check your answer. The first one has been done for you.

| | | |
|---|---|---|
| **1.** $x - 5 = 14$<br>$x - 5 + 5 = 14 + 5$<br>$x = 19$<br><br>**Check:**<br>$19 - 5 = 14$<br>$14 = 14$ | **2.** $x - 7 = 25$<br><br><br><br>**Check:** | **3.** $7 + x = 19$<br><br><br><br>**Check:** |
| **4.** $x - 4 = 20$<br><br><br><br>**Check:** | **5.** $8 + x = 15$<br><br><br><br>**Check:** | **6.** $9 + x = 9$<br><br><br><br>**Check:** |
| **7.** $x + 6 = 12$<br><br><br><br>**Check:** | **8.** $x - 12 = 17$<br><br><br><br>**Check:** | **9.** $15 + x = 31$<br><br><br><br>**Check:** |

# Practice 35

**Directions:** Rewrite each problem and solve. The first one has been done for you.

$$n = 10$$

**1.** 2 x *n* = _____2 x 10 = 20_____

**2.** *n* − 5 = _____

**3.** 3 + *n* = _____

**4.** 3 x *n* = _____

**5.** *n* ÷ 2 = _____

**6.** 9 x *n* = _____

**7.** *n* − 1 = _____

**8.** *n* − 8 = _____

**9.** 8 + *n* = _____

**10.** *n* ÷ 5 = _____

**Directions:** Add the missing sign (+, −, x, ÷) to make each equation true. Rewrite the equation and solve. The first one has been done for you.

$$s = 9$$

**11.** *s* __÷__ 3 = 3 _____9 ÷ 3 = 3_____

**12.** *s* _____ 1 = 9 _____

**13.** 4 _____ *s* = 36 _____

**14.** *s* _____ 7 = 2 _____

**15.** *s* _____ 8 = 1 _____

**16.** *s* _____ 8 = 72 _____

**17.** *s* _____ 10 = 19 _____

**18.** *s* _____ 1 = 9 _____

**19.** *s* _____ 9 = 1 _____

**20.** 5 _____ *s* = 14 _____

# Practice 36

**Directions:** Write the coordinate for each point.

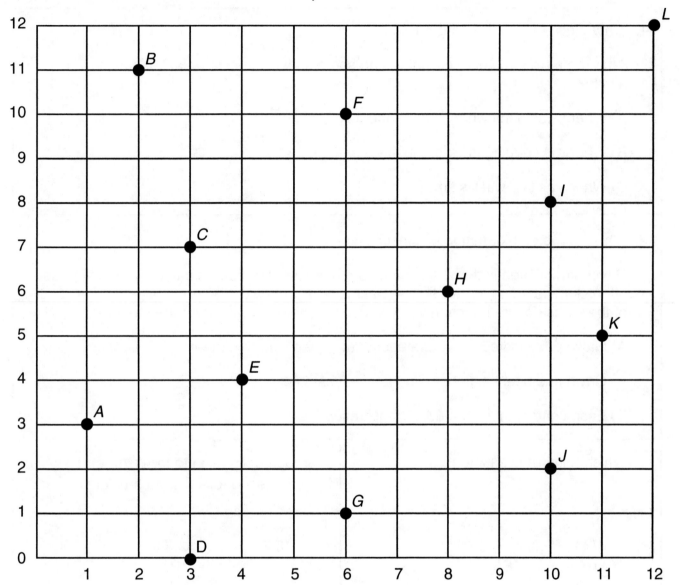

**1.** $K =$ _____      **4.** $L =$ _____      **7.** $H =$ _____      **10.** $C =$ _____

**2.** $D =$ _____      **5.** $E =$ _____      **8.** $B =$ _____      **11.** $A =$ _____

**3.** $G =$ _____      **6.** $I =$ _____      **9.** $F =$ _____      **12.** $J =$ _____

# Test Practice 1

**Directions:** Fill in the correct answer circle.

---

**1.** What piece of information is missing?

Jana ran a mile 10 seconds faster than she did last week. How fast can Jana run a mile?

Ⓐ Where was Jana when she ran the mile?

Ⓑ Who was keeping track of the time?

Ⓒ What was last week's time?

---

**2.** Which piece of information is unnecessary?

Gavin participated in the skateboarding rodeo with 315 other contestants. Gavin has been skateboarding for five years. Each contestant paid a $7.50 registration fee. Half of the fee is donated to charity. How much money was raised for the charity?

Ⓐ Gavin participated in the skateboarding rodeo with 315 other contestants.

Ⓑ Gavin has been skateboarding for five years.

Ⓒ Each contestant paid a $7.50 registration fee.

---

**3.** Which number is an integer?

| 27 1/2 | ⁻27 | .27 |
|--------|-----|-----|
| Ⓐ | Ⓑ | Ⓒ |

**4.** Use estimation to the nearest ten thousand to solve the problem.

$$32,539 + 34,713$$

| 60,000 | 50,000 | 65,000 |
|--------|--------|--------|
| Ⓐ | Ⓑ | Ⓒ |

---

**5.** Which number is written correctly?

| 81,814,181,0.543 | 81814,1810,543 | 818,141,810,543 |
|------------------|----------------|-----------------|
| Ⓐ | Ⓑ | Ⓒ |

# Test Practice 2

**Directions:** Fill in the correct answer circle.

---

**1.** Which one has the integers in correct sequential order?

Ⓐ  3, ⁻10, ⁻9, 2, 10, ⁻6

Ⓑ  ⁻6, ⁻9, ⁻10, 2, 3, 10

Ⓒ  ⁻10, ⁻9, ⁻6, 2, 3, 10

---

**2.** Solve the problem.

$$^-92 - {}^-5 = \underline{\quad\quad}$$

⁻97          ⁻87          ⁺87

Ⓐ            Ⓑ            Ⓒ

---

**3.** Find the least common multiple for 7 and 12.

19            24            84

Ⓐ            Ⓑ            Ⓒ

---

**4.** Add.

$$2\ 1/8 + 8\ 4/8 = \underline{\quad\quad}$$

10/8        16 5/8        10 5/8

Ⓐ            Ⓑ            Ⓒ

---

**5.** Subtract.

$$8\ 6/7 - 6\ 2/7 = \underline{\quad\quad}$$

2 4/7        14 4/7        2 7/7

Ⓐ            Ⓑ            Ⓒ

---

**6.** Add.

$$9\ 5/6 + 7\ 2/6 = \underline{\quad\quad}$$

2 3/6        16 3/6        17 1/6

Ⓐ            Ⓑ            Ⓒ

---

**7.** Subtract.

$$7\ 1/10 - 5\ 5/10 = \underline{\quad\quad}$$

3 3/5        1 3/5        12 3/5

Ⓐ            Ⓑ            Ⓒ

---

**8.** Multiply.

$$237 \times 1{,}000 = \underline{\quad\quad}$$

2,370        23,700        237,000

Ⓐ            Ⓑ            Ⓒ

---

**9.** Pencils sell for $1.39 a box. Jeffrey buys 17 boxes. How much money does he need to pay for the pencils?

$23.63                $17.63                $63.19

Ⓐ                    Ⓑ                    Ⓒ

---

# Test Practice 3

**Directions:** Fill in the correct answer circle.

| | |
|---|---|
| **1.** Find the product.<br><br>$615 \times 62 = \underline{\hspace{1cm}}$<br><br>3,813     38,130     381,300<br>Ⓐ       Ⓑ       Ⓒ | **2.** Find the product.<br><br>$2,844 \times 749 = \underline{\hspace{1cm}}$<br><br>2,130,156   213,015.6   213,015<br>Ⓐ       Ⓑ       Ⓒ |
| **3.** Find the quotient.<br><br>$11\overline{)1,079}$<br><br>19 R8     98 R1     89 R1<br>Ⓐ       Ⓑ       Ⓒ | **4.** Find the quotient.<br><br>$39\overline{)79,510}$<br><br>2,803 R28   2,038 R28   2,083 R82<br>Ⓐ       Ⓑ       Ⓒ |
| **5.** How many seconds are in 4 1/2 minutes?<br><br>240     270     740<br>Ⓐ       Ⓑ       Ⓒ | **6.** How many minutes are in 6 1/4 hours?<br><br>360     375     400<br>Ⓐ       Ⓑ       Ⓒ |
| **7.** How many inches are in 3 1/3 feet?<br><br>40"     43"     46"<br>Ⓐ       Ⓑ       Ⓒ | **8.** How many inches are in 1 1/3 yards?<br><br>36"     48"     60"<br>Ⓐ       Ⓑ       Ⓒ |
| **9.** How many feet are in 7 yards?<br><br>10 feet     7 feet     21 feet<br>Ⓐ       Ⓑ       Ⓒ | **10.** How many yards are in 10 feet?<br><br>3 1/2     3 1/3     3 2/3<br>Ⓐ       Ⓑ       Ⓒ |

 #3746 Practice Makes Perfect: Math Review     © Teacher Created Resources, Inc.

# Test Practice 4

**Directions:** Fill in the correct answer circle.

## Jumping Jacks

The members in Troop 87 did as many jumping jacks as they possibly could in 2 minutes. Below are the results.

| | | | | | |
|---|---|---|---|---|---|
| Abe | 110 | Bethany | 95 | Chris | 29 |
| Donna | 48 | Eric | 86 | Frieda | 66 |
| George | 26 | Hannah | 77 | Ivan | 71 |
| Jane | 56 | | | | |

**1.** What was the average number of jumping jacks completed?

| 60.4 | 63.4 | 66.4 |
|---|---|---|
| Ⓐ | Ⓑ | Ⓒ |

**2.** What was the median number of jumping jacks completed by the members?

| 68.5 | 65.8 | 58.6 |
|---|---|---|
| Ⓐ | Ⓑ | Ⓒ |

**3.** What was the mode for the number of jumping jacks completed by each member?

| Not Applicable | 0 | 56 |
|---|---|---|
| Ⓐ | Ⓑ | Ⓒ |

**4.** Solve.

$$(45 + {}^-23) \times 7 = \underline{\qquad}$$

| $^-476$ | $^-154$ | 154 |
|---|---|---|
| Ⓐ | Ⓑ | Ⓒ |

**5.** Find the value.

$$9^2 = \underline{\qquad}$$

| 81 | 11 | 74 |
|---|---|---|
| Ⓐ | Ⓑ | Ⓒ |

**6.** Solve.

$$(5^2 + 6^2) + (3 \div 1) = \underline{\qquad}$$

| 62 | 63 | 64 |
|---|---|---|
| Ⓐ | Ⓑ | Ⓒ |

**7.** Which one is true?

| $8^2 = 4^3$ | $8^2 = 4 \times 3$ | $8 \times 8 \times 8 = 4^3$ |
|---|---|---|
| Ⓐ | Ⓑ | Ⓒ |

# Test Practice 5

**Directions:** Fill in the correct answer circle.

---

**1.** Dolly had 3 hits out of 7 at bats. What is her batting average?

| .429 | 4.29 | 42.9 |
|:---:|:---:|:---:|
| Ⓐ | Ⓑ | Ⓒ |

**2.** Jason spelled 8 out of 11 spelling words correctly. What was his spelling score? (Round the score to the nearest whole number.)

| 72% | 73% | 74% |
|:---:|:---:|:---:|
| Ⓐ | Ⓑ | Ⓒ |

---

**3.** Which number is the same as 15%?

| 15.0 | 1.50 | .150 |
|:---:|:---:|:---:|
| Ⓐ | Ⓑ | Ⓒ |

**4.** What is the fraction for .75?

| 7/5 | 3/4 | 5/7 |
|:---:|:---:|:---:|
| Ⓐ | Ⓑ | Ⓒ |

---

**5.** To pass the driving test, Jamal needs to have a score of at least 60%. If there are 25 questions on the test, how many must Jamal answer correctly?

| 14 | 15 | 16 |
|:---:|:---:|:---:|
| Ⓐ | Ⓑ | Ⓒ |

**6.** The Friendly Bank pays 2% interest each month on each account. Cassie has $200 in her account. With interest, what will her total amount be at the end of the month?

| $202.00 | $204.00 | $200.40 |
|:---:|:---:|:---:|
| Ⓐ | Ⓑ | Ⓒ |

---

**7.** What is the rate?

Skippy can pack 10 bags of peanuts for every 8 boxes Jiffy opens.

| 10 to 8 | 4 to 5 | 8 to 3 |
|:---:|:---:|:---:|
| Ⓐ | Ⓑ | Ⓒ |

**8.** Connie can scoop 3 scoops of ice cream every 8 seconds. How many whole scoops can Connie scoop in 1 minute?

| 22 | 25 | 23 |
|:---:|:---:|:---:|
| Ⓐ | Ⓑ | Ⓒ |

---

# Test Practice 6

**Directions:** Fill in the correct answer circle.

| Volume Formulas | |
| --- | --- |
| sphere | $4/3 \times \pi \times r^3$ = cubic units |
| cube | $s^3$ = cubic units |
| rectangular solid | $l \times w \times h$ = cubic units |
| cylinder | $\pi \times r^2 \times h$ = cubic units |

**1.** Find the volume of the cube.

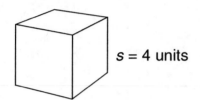

$s = 4$ units

   16 c.u.       12 c.u.       64 c.u.

   Ⓐ         Ⓑ         Ⓒ

**2.** Name the angle.

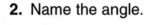

  ∠ABC       ∠BAC       ∠CAB

   Ⓐ         Ⓑ         Ⓒ

**3.** Identify the triangle.

  scalene      isosceles      equilateral

   Ⓐ         Ⓑ         Ⓒ

**4.** Identify the lines.

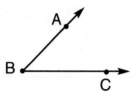

  adjacent      intersecting      perpendicular

   Ⓐ         Ⓑ         Ⓒ

**5.** Measure the angle.

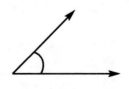

  75°        45°        60°

   Ⓐ         Ⓑ         Ⓒ

**6.** Solve for *n*.

$$n - 14 = 10$$

  26         22         24

   Ⓐ         Ⓑ         Ⓒ

# Answer Sheet

| **Test Practice 1** (Page 40) | **Test Practice 2** (Page 41) | **Test Practice 3** (Page 42) |
|---|---|---|
| 1. Ⓐ Ⓑ Ⓒ | 1. Ⓐ Ⓑ Ⓒ | 1. Ⓐ Ⓑ Ⓒ |
| 2. Ⓐ Ⓑ Ⓒ | 2. Ⓐ Ⓑ Ⓒ | 2. Ⓐ Ⓑ Ⓒ |
| 3. Ⓐ Ⓑ Ⓒ | 3. Ⓐ Ⓑ Ⓒ | 3. Ⓐ Ⓑ Ⓒ |
| 4. Ⓐ Ⓑ Ⓒ | 4. Ⓐ Ⓑ Ⓒ | 4. Ⓐ Ⓑ Ⓒ |
| 5. Ⓐ Ⓑ Ⓒ | 5. Ⓐ Ⓑ Ⓒ | 5. Ⓐ Ⓑ Ⓒ |
| | 6. Ⓐ Ⓑ Ⓒ | 6. Ⓐ Ⓑ Ⓒ |
| | 7. Ⓐ Ⓑ Ⓒ | 7. Ⓐ Ⓑ Ⓒ |
| | 8. Ⓐ Ⓑ Ⓒ | 8. Ⓐ Ⓑ Ⓒ |
| | 9. Ⓐ Ⓑ Ⓒ | 9. Ⓐ Ⓑ Ⓒ |
| | | 10. Ⓐ Ⓑ Ⓒ |

| **Test Practice 4** (Page 43) | **Test Practice 5** (Page 44) | **Test Practice 6** (Page 45) |
|---|---|---|
| 1. Ⓐ Ⓑ Ⓒ | 1. Ⓐ Ⓑ Ⓒ | 1. Ⓐ Ⓑ Ⓒ |
| 2. Ⓐ Ⓑ Ⓒ | 2. Ⓐ Ⓑ Ⓒ | 2. Ⓐ Ⓑ Ⓒ |
| 3. Ⓐ Ⓑ Ⓒ | 3. Ⓐ Ⓑ Ⓒ | 3. Ⓐ Ⓑ Ⓒ |
| 4. Ⓐ Ⓑ Ⓒ | 4. Ⓐ Ⓑ Ⓒ | 4. Ⓐ Ⓑ Ⓒ |
| 5. Ⓐ Ⓑ Ⓒ | 5. Ⓐ Ⓑ Ⓒ | 5. Ⓐ Ⓑ Ⓒ |
| 6. Ⓐ Ⓑ Ⓒ | 6. Ⓐ Ⓑ Ⓒ | 6. Ⓐ Ⓑ Ⓒ |
| 7. Ⓐ Ⓑ Ⓒ | 7. Ⓐ Ⓑ Ⓒ | |
| | 8. Ⓐ Ⓑ Ⓒ | |

# Answer Key ꩜ ꩜ ꩜ ꩜ ꩜ ꩜ ꩜ ꩜ ꩜ ꩜ ꩜ ꩜ ꩜

**Page 4**
1. How many friends did Betsy invite?
2. How many hens are there?
3. How many miles is it from David's house to the beach?
4. What is Suzanne's weekly allowance?
5. How many students are in the class?
6. How many days are in the month?
7. How many markers are in each box?
8. How much does a cup of coffee cost?

**Page 5**
1. Cross out: His favorite flavor of dog bones is peanut butter; 210
2. Cross out: $500 in nickels; $8,000
3. Cross out: The stadium was beautifully decorated; $900
4. Cross out: The parking garage was built in 1950; 1,584

**Page 6**
1. 2,774,385
2. 465,103,181
3. 25,868,107,559
4. 941,174,744,610
5. 371,016,971
6. 6,291,246,628
7. 2,986,954,931
8. 712,431,664
9. 429,101,565,486
10. 725,108,328,514
11. 897,129,184,110
12. 107,772,106,761
13. 300,000,000,000 + 30,000,000,000 + 1,000,000,000 + 900,000,000 + 30,000,000 + 8,000,000 + 500,000 + 40,000 + 7,000 + 400 + 40 + 6
14. 600,000,000,000 + 90,000,000,000 + 5,000,000,000 + 600,000,000 + 60,000,000 + 5,000,000 + 800,000 + 30,000 + 9,000 + 700 + 20

**Page 7**
1. Actual: 124,427
   Estimated: 70,000 + 60,000 = 130,000
   Yes
2. Actual: 63,549 − 55,318 = 8,231
   Estimated: 60,000 − 60,000 = 0
   No
3. Actual: 77,352 + 31,166 = 108,518
   Estimated: 80,000 + 30,000 = 110,000
   Yes
4. Actual: 88,818 − 8,167 = 80,651
   Estimated: 90,000 − 10,000 = 80,000
   Yes

**Page 8**
1. 17
2. −54, −61, 25
3. −19
4. 40, −29, 98
5. +7
6. −5
7. +1
8. +6
9. +9
10. +2
11. −5
12. −1

**Page 9**
Number Line: −10, −9, −8, (−7), −6, −5, −4, −3, (−2), −1, (0), 1, 2, 3, (4), 5, 6, 7, 8, 9, (10)
1. −9, −7, −4, −3, 5
2. −3, −1, 5, 8, 9
3. −10, −6, −3, 1, 3
4. −8, −2, 0, 4, 5
5. −9, −8, −6, 1, 2
6. −7, −6, −1, 3, 4
7. −6, −5, 0, 2, 10

**Page 10**
Circle: 1, 2, 5, 9, 10
Underline: 15, 18, 23
25. −3
26. −12
27. −17
28. 2
29. −5
30. 4
31. 17
32. 5
33. −15
34. −5
35. 3
36. 6
37. 14
38. −10
39. −7
40. −1
41. 0
42. 11

**Page 11**
1. 5: 5, 10, 15, 20, 25, 30
   6: 6, 12, 18, 24, 30
   LCM = 30
2. 3: 3, 6, 9, 12, 15, 18, 21
   7: 7, 14, 21
   LCM = 21
3. 8: 8, 16, 24, 32, 40, 48, 56, 64, 72
   9: 9, 18, 27, 36, 45, 54, 63, 72
   LCM = 72
4. 9: 3 x 3
   14: 2 x 7
   LCM = 126
5. 12: 2 x 2 x 3
   5: 5 x 1
   LCM = 60
6. 10: 2 x 5
   3: 1 x 3
   LCM = 30
7. 15: 3 x 5
   2: 2 x 1
   LCM = 30
8. 8: 2 x 2 x 2
   21: 3 x 7
   LCM = 168

**Page 12**
1. 5 4/5
2. 15
3. 15 3/5
4. 3 2/3
5. 3 3/8
6. 12
7. 3 2/9
8. 11 4/5
9. 5 1/2

**Page 13**
1. 13/30
2. 3/8
3. 17/36
4. 21/22
5. 9/22
6. 1 31/88
7. 7/20
8. 1 5/12
9. 3 41/42
10. 53/84
11. 4 1/4
12. 7 1/30
13. 13 1/35
14. 3/4
15. 5 1/12
16. 11 27/35

**Page 14**
1. 61,000
2. 300
3. 7,240
4. 5,600
5. 91,800
6. 5,710
7. 385,000
8. 41,000
9. 726,000
10. 8,810
11. 37,000
12. 9,000
13. 0

**Page 9 (continued)**
Mystery message:
Multiplying by tens is easy!
14. >
15. <
16. >
17. >
18. <
19. <

**Page 15**
1. 58,072
2. 2,516
3. 986
4. 642,873
5. 32,824
6. 21,033
7. 2,277
8. 109,272
9. 3,634,770
10. 43,183
11. 19,241
12. 950,544

**Page 16**
1. 54,132
2. 288,184
3. 132,948
4. 74,808
5. 4,722,070
6. 44,042,130
7. 17,710,528
8. 51,298,965
9. 26,896,941

**Page 17**
1. 8,400 ÷ 40 = 210
   Check: 210 x 40 = 8,400
2. 41,916 ÷ 28 = 1,497
   Check: 1,497 x 28 = 41,916
3. 33,320 ÷ 136 = 245
   Check: 245 x 136 = 33,320
4. 3,600 ÷ 90 = 40
   Check: 40 x 90 = 3,600
5. 8,928 ÷ 9 = 992
   Check: 992 x 9 = 8,928
6. 28,917 ÷ 81 = 357
   Check: 357 x 81 = 28,917
7. 35,620 ÷ 260 = 137
   Check: 137 x 260 = 35,620
8. 180,930 ÷ 37 = 4,890
   Check: 4,890 x 37 = 180,930
9. 8,840 ÷ 65 = 136
   Check: 136 x 65 = 8,840

**Page 18**
1. 643 R65
2. 2,808 R6
3. 1,927 R6
4. 1,827 R5
5. 3,876 R1
6. 1,102 R82
7. 118 R572
8. 32 R56
9. 141 R109
10. 1,396 R69
11. 552 R62
12. 7,748 R277
13. 3,252 R5
14. 136 R219
15. 7,126 R64
16. 12,400 R106

**Page 19**
1. 15 minutes/900 seconds
2. 30 minutes/1,800 seconds
3. 45 minutes/2,700 seconds
4. 60 minutes/3,600 seconds
5. 120 minutes/7,200 seconds
6. 180 minutes/10,800 seconds
7. 240 minutes/14,400 seconds
8. 360 minutes/21,600 seconds
9. 480 minutes/28,800 seconds
10. 720 minutes/43,200 seconds
11. 1,080 minutes/64,800 seconds
12. 1,440 minutes/86,400 seconds
13. >
14. <
15. >
16. >

# Answer Key

## Page 20
1. 84
2. 60
3. 24
4. 120
5. 66
6. 27
7. 78
8. 68
9. 8
10. 1
11. 2
12. 4
13. 5 2/3
14. 1/2
15. 2 1/2
16. 4 1/2
17. 8
18. 2
19. 4
20. 2 1/3
21. 2
22. 1

## Page 21
1. $5.60    $6.50

## Page 22
1. $9.00
2. The average weekly allowance would increase.
3. There would be two modes: $5.00 and $10.00.

## Page 23
1. 10 + 16 = 26
2. 3 + 26 = 29
3. 2 – 2 = 0
4. 3 + 9 – 10 = 2
5. 5 + 42 – 3 = 44
6. 20 + 3 – 4 = 19
7. (16 + 5) ÷ 3 = 7
8. 17 – (9 – 4) = 12
9. 1 + 36 = 37
10. (3 x 3) – 7 = 2
11. 8 (1) + 2 = 10
12. 16 + 27 – 40 = 3

## Page 24
1. 13%
2. 33%
3. 89%
4. 17%
5. 50%
6. 86%
7. 29%
8. 80%
9. Eric
10. Josh
11. 3
12. 2
13. 3
14. 7

## Page 25
1. 4
2. 9
3. 6
4. 5
5. 36
6. 6
7. 9
8. 2
9. 5
10. 13
11. 8
12. 11

## Page 26
1. $45.00
2. $1,545.00
3. 0
4. 0
5. Lee didn't earn any money because the balance was not high enough.
6. $3.50
7. $353.50
8. $150.00
9. $5,150.00

## Page 27
1. Month 2: ($550,00), + $110.00, –$50.00, $610.00
   Month 3: $610.00, + $122.00, – $50.00, $682.00
   Month 4: $682.00, + $136.40, – $50.00, $768.40
   Month 5: $768.40
2. He would never pay off the balance. The balance would continue to increase.
3. No, the payments aren't big enough. The balance would continue to increase.
4. $468.40

## Page 28
1. Month 2: ($400.00), $80.00, – $200.00, $280.00
   Month 3: $280.00, $56.00, – $200.00, $136.00
   Month 4: $136.00, $27.20, – $200.00, 0
   Month 5: 0
2. $263.20
3. $763.20
4. $107.75
5. $155.45

## Page 29
1. 2, 3
   4, 6
   6, 9
   8, 12
   10, 15
   12, 18
2. 5, 12
   10, 24
   15, 36
   20, 48
   25, 60
   30, 72
3. 30, 10
   60, 20
   90, 30
   120, 40
   150, 50
   180, 60
3. 3, 2
   6, 4
   9, 6
   12, 8
   15, 10
   18, 12

## Page 30
1. 150
2. 5
3. 8
4. 2 1/2
5. 12.41
6. 6

## Page 31
1. 7 x 5 x 7 = 245 cubic units
2. 6 x 4 x 5 = 120 cubic units
3. 3 x 1 x 6 = 18 cubic units
4. $1^3$ = 1 cubic unit
5. $7^3$ = 343 cubic units
6. $5^3$ = 125 cubic units

## Page 32
1. 28.26
2. 62.8
3. 1,230.88
4. 904.32
5. 33.49
6. 267.94

## Page 33
1. acute = angle less than 90°
2. equilateral = three congruent sides
3. isosceles = two congruent sides
4. obtuse = angle more than 90°
5. right = 90° angle
6. scalene = no congruent sides
7. isosceles, right
8. scalene, obtuse
9. equilateral, acute

## Page 34
1. 70°
2. 10°
3. 180°
4. 80°
5. 95°
6. 135°
7. 90°
8. 165°
9. 30°

## Page 35
1. ∠ABC, ∠CBA
2. ∠DEF, ∠FED
3. ∠GHI, ∠IHJ
4. ∠JKL and ∠LKM
5. ∠NOP and ∠POQ
6. ∠RST and ∠TSU
7. perpendicular
8. intersecting
9. perpendicular
10. complementary
11. supplementary

## Page 36 Check angles for correct measurements.

## Page 37
1. $x - 5 + 5 = 14 + 5$
   $x = 19$
   Check: $19 - 5 = 14$
2. $x - 7 + 7 = 25 + 7$
   $x = 32$
   Check: $32 - 7 = 25$
3. $7 - 7 + x = 19 - 7$
   $x = 12$
   Check: $7 + 12 = 19$
4. $x - 4 + 4 = 20 + 4$
   $x = 24$
   Check: $24 - 4 = 20$
5. $8 - 8 + x = 15 - 8$
   $x = 7$
   Check: $8 + 7 = 15$
6. $9 - 9 + x = 9 - 9$
   $x = 0$
   Check: $9 + 0 = 9$
7. $x + 6 - 6 = 12 - 6$
   $x = 6$
   Check: $6 + 6 = 12$
8. $x - 12 + 12 = 17 + 12$
   $x = 29$
   Check: $29 - 12 = 17$
9. $15 - 15 + x = 31 - 15$
   $x = 16$
   Check: $15 + 16 = 31$

## Page 38
1. 2 x 10 = 20
2. 10 – 5 = 5
3. 3 + 10 = 13
4. 3 x 10 = 30
5. 10 ÷ 2 = 5
6. 9 x 10 = 90
7. 10 – 1 = 9
8. 10 – 8 = 2
9. 8 + 10 = 18
10. 10 ÷ 5 = 2
11. 9 ÷ 3 = 3
12. 9 x (or ÷)1 = 9
13. 4 x 9 = 36
14. 9 – 7 = 2
15. 9 – 8 = 1
16. 9 x 8 = 72
17. 9 + 10 = 19
18. 9 x (or ÷)1 = 9
19. 9 ÷ 9 = 1
20. 5 + 9 = 14

## Page 39
1. (11, 5)
2. (3, 0)
3. (6, 1)
4. (12, 12)
5. (4, 4)
6. (10, 8)
7. (8, 6)
8. (2, 11)
9. (6, 10)
10. (3, 7)
11. (1, 3)
12. (10, 2)

## Page 40
1. C
2. B
3. B
4. A
5. C

## Page 41
1. C
2. B
3. C
4. C
5. A
6. C
7. B
8. C
9. A

## Page 42
1. B
2. A
3. B
4. B
5. B
6. B
7. A
8. B
9. C
10. B

## Page 43
1. C
2. A
3. A
4. C
5. A
6. C
7. A

## Page 44
1. A
2. B
3. C
4. B
5. B
6. B
7. A
8. A

## Page 45
1. C
2. A
3. C
4. B
5. B
6. C